COUNTRY HOMES

This 2007 edition published by Barnes & Noble, Inc.
by arrangement with Hachette Filipacchi Media U.S., Inc..

Translated by Simon Pleasance and Fronza Woods
Edited by Jennifer Ladonne
Art direction by Pascal Fromont

ISBN-13: 978-0-7607-9093-9
ISBN-10: 0-7607-9093-0

Printed and bound in China

10 9 8 7 6 5 4 3 2 1

COUNTRY HOMES

Elegant weekend
retreats from
around the world

JEAN DEMACHY

Text by Olivier de Vleeschouwer

BARNES
& NOBLE
NEW YORK

CONTENTS

INTRODUCTION

No matter what the season, there is something amazingly seductive about the idea of getting away to a weekend house. The nonstop hustle and bustle of city life may be intoxicating during the week, but true pleasure is to be found in escaping to the country, near or far, whether for a couple of days or a proper restorative holiday. And not surprisingly, given the element of escapism involved, country houses are often packed with more character and feeling than their urban counterparts; a city apartment can be a refuge come six o'clock, but a weekend place is where you go to breathe, to relax, to recharge. In short, it's where you find yourself again. In "Country Homes: Elegant Weekend Retreats From Around the World," editor extraordinaire Jean Demachy skillfully culls the most intriguing and entrancing country houses from the pages of ELLE DECO magazines around the world. The characteristics they share? Smart design and dazzling style.

Demachy's selections — faithful to the ELLE DECO tradition of showcasing homes packed with ideas and inspiration — include the charming Sussex farmhouse of designer John Stefanidis, fashion powerhouse Pierre Bergé's breathtakingly chic retreat in Saint-Rémy-de-Provence, tastemaker Axel Vervoordt's eclectic Antwerp castle, and a striking Modernist glass pavilion by Thomas Phifer and Muriel Brandolini in New York's historic Hudson River Valley. The exquisite photographs of living rooms, bedrooms, kitchens, gardens, and swimming pools are tantalizing; you can practically catch the sweet scent of lavender in the breeze. From rustic cabins to stately manors to barefoot beach cottages, these are houses with emotional resonance. Their rooms have a bit of patina and heaps of personality. Best of all, they have been created with confidence by talented, stylish people as the backdrop to lives well lived — just like yours.

Margaret Russell
editor in chief, ELLE DECOR

OPPOSITE
The garden gives pride of place to flowers in
white, Julie Prisca's favorites. In the midst of
symmetrical, box-lined squares, aromatic
herbs are within easy reach of the kitchen.
The four buildings surrounding the garden
lend it a much-appreciated privacy.

Cottages

THE DISCREET ALLURE OF
ENGLISH-STYLE DECORATION

*These singular homes do not harbor visions of grandeur. They are resolutely rustic,
and have that good-natured simplicity that seems to put them on intimate terms with
the birds, bees and, most of all, flowers. For some, you must duck your head a
bit to get into the converted attic. Yet one happily complies; for these rural beauties
aspire to nothing more than their own idiosyncratic style. Cottage owners cherish
no illusions about their particular status. They're content to have finally found
a quiet place where simplicity can flourish in the most surprising ways.
Their personal vision — which never rules out originality or daring — insures
homes of great originality that may also resemble the ideal of a happy household.*

COUNTRYSIDE AT THE GATES OF PARIS

To summon the sun in Normandy, where she now lives all year round, home furnishings designer Julie Prisca painted the walls of her old post house with warm southern colors. In this bright and luminous atmosphere, Prisca finds many a source of inspiration through the large windows looking out over a delightful walled garden.

OPPOSITE
The only room in the house that features neutral shades, this large attic bedroom displays some of Julie's own creations, like the big zinc-and-glass lamp and amusing Medici-style vase made of chicken wire.

BELOW
Adjoining the bedroom, the attic bathroom is a showcase for natural materials. The basin surround is in beech wood. The mirror on its iron verdigris stand was also designed by the mistress of the house.

Normandy, France

OPPOSITE
The provocative tones of the living room are a perfect antidote to Normandy's ever-changing skies. Saffron walls, green beams, cockscomb red sofa and steely blue armchairs all converge to form an optimistic whole that brightens at the least change of light.

BELOW
This symphony of colors begins in the entrance hall, where visitors are treated to an invigorating assortment of hues. The paneled stairway wall was painted lagoon green and the ceiling a deeper teal.

A VILLAGE RESIDENCE DONE ON ENGLISH TIME

Because haste is not a typically British trait, the owner of this Elizabethan house preferred to live in it before plunging into all the restoration work that he nonetheless deemed vital. This was the only way, in his view, to make a successful renovation well in tune with the spirit of the place. The happy outcome supports this prudent theory.

OPPOSITE
In agreement with his architect Anthony Matthes, the owner Brian Godbold decided to add a small building on the garden side that now acts as greenhouse and shed. This Suffolk home has thus gained in both volume and character.

ABOVE
The master of the house has a special preference for low-ceilinged bedrooms,
which guarantee intimacy. In this bedroom, the walls are covered with a classic
blue-striped wallpaper (Colefax & Fowler). The twin 19th-century iron beds, picked
up in a local antique shop, bring a sense of order and harmony to the room.

OPPOSITE
Everything in this bedroom is neatly matched at dignified right angles.
The stately Empire bed has a bedside table from the same period. On the
mahogany chest of drawers rest two fine copper oil lamps.

Suffolk, England

BELOW

Warm-hearted simplicity is the theme for this eat-in kitchen. A pleasing harmony prevails between the mellow pine furniture and the deeper tones of the earthenware dishes typical to the south of France. The master of the house evidently means to capture every last drop of warmth for this cheerful room.

OPPOSITE

A pedestal washbasin for each side of an elegant, wood-encased bathtub. To enhance the perfect symmetry of the decor, each basin has its own identical round mirror, intentionally diminutive to convey a feeling of intimacy. The armchair, covered in a muted striped fabric by Charles Hammond, and a soft-hued rug help give this room its comfortable, old-fashioned appeal.

FOLLOWING SPREAD
Hanging above the gas-fueled fireplace a pair of "forebears"—found in a secondhand store—keep stern watch over the living room, most likely approving of its very British atmosphere. A leather chesterfield is perfect for engulfing one luxuriously during long hours of reading and relaxation.

PEACE AND QUIET ON A RIVERSIDE NEAR PARIS

The owners have made the very most of this large cottage-style house set alongside a riverbank. Its potential was obvious, but not without certain shortcomings. By adding extra windows, combining clear, bright colors, and marrying antique and contemporary furniture, the architect transformed this home into a lively symbol of Ile-de-France style.

OPPOSITE
On the garden side, walls were erected to create a pleasant area for relaxation, with a handsome graveled walk bisecting the close-cropped lawn. Because the façade was windowless, apertures were made to bring more light inside.

BELOW
In the inner courtyard, beneath a rebuilt roof, a large table welcomes friends who are always more than happy to make the most of this shady spot, cool even on hot summer days.

Ile-de-France, France

OPPOSITE

A series of low hedges designate the garden plots. In the kitchen garden, flowers and vegetables alternate inside box-hemmed rectangles. Waiting for the harvest season, old cloches and espaliered fruit trees create winningly charming scenes.

BELOW

Jars of jam, barbotine ware and a collection of antique pitchers: a pretty still life that truly transcends time.

OPPOSITE

All pink and petals, this bedroom is a celebration of
feminine refinement, all the more lovely for its cozy sitting-
room nook. Flowery chintz fabric, dressing table
and an armchair with ruffled skirt come together with
a subtle plaid-covered daybed to create an updated
version of a beloved classic.

BELOW

In the hall, watering cans signify gardens—a central motif
in this home. The console and pale wooden lamps were
designed by the architect for the David Hicks Boutique.

AN AESTHETE'S ENCLAVE WITHIN RHAPSODIES OF GREEN

Under the Sussex sky, architect and decorator John Stefanidis cultivates his serious yet spontaneous love of gardening. His passion is such that in the space of just a few years, this modest farm has nearly vanished beneath an amazing profusion of spheres, pyramids and rectangles of green, giving his English retreat a continental flavor, half French, half Italian.

OPPOSITE
All around the house, John Stefanidis installed a series of small enclosures where flowers and shrubs extend a leafy invitation to meditate, read or just rest the eyes.

FOLLOWING SPREAD
The old stables were transformed into a large living room whose brick walls were painted matte white. The gentle lighting is the subtle result of screens filtering daylight through old windows. Here all the materials are natural, imparting an atmosphere of softness and comfort.

Sussex, England

ABOVE
Over the years, trimmed hornbeam, box and yew have grown up to
create dense and mysterious enclosures behind narrow painted gates. No nook
in this garden has escaped the owner's magic touch.

OPPOSITE
In this cozy living room, everything harmonizes for a rose-colored view of comfort.
Plain, floral and striped fabrics blend to give the room a poetic air.

OPPOSITE
Two facing stables were transformed into a
wood-beamed greenhouse topped
with a soaring pinnacle and housing lush,
cascading vines. Here again, the space is
demarcated by carefully manicured bushes
and exuberant banks of roses.

FOLLOWING SPREAD
This part of the garden gives a clear glimpse
of the ease with which the house seems
to surrender to the voluptuous weight of
blooms. John Stefanidis admits to an unbridled
adoration for roses which, nonetheless, make
room for stands of tentacled yellow mullein.

EARTH TONES AND FLOWERS FOR A GUEST HOUSE OF RARE DELIGHT

Surrounded by 300-year-old trees, the Norman abode that Pierre Brinon fell in love with is now a guest house in a league of its own, thanks to his keen eye and inimitable sense of hospitality. In this ample 19th-century building, constructed over the ruins of a castle, inventiveness is notable in each and every detail.

OPPOSITE
The owner's flair is not limited to decorating, his sizable kitchen puts forth fabulous feasts of his own devising. With its pink-brick walls, textured plaster ceiling and large slate floor tiles, this room makes cooking an inspired event enjoyed by one and all.

BELOW
Missing drawers in this seed cupboard were replaced by apples, which scent the entire room with the aroma of sunny orchards.

Normandy, France

OPPOSITE

The guest bedroom's high ceilings were cleverly accentuated by extending its white borders one-quarter down the wall. An unexpected stand-in for a headboard, equestrian enthusiasts will recognize a genuine saddle-rack.

BELOW

The inventiveness displayed in each nook and cranny is highlighted by the eclectic combinations that are its hallmark. Walls covered in raw linen go well with the hyacinth-blue woodwork. On an old offertory box, Pierre Brinon assembled a collection of zinc objects of all shapes and styles.

FOLLOWING SPREAD

The surprising corridor leading to the bedrooms on the second floor plays on an innovative juxtaposition of patterns, from floral to geometric. Not an experiment for the faint-hearted, but remarkably effective in its audaciousness. Brinon heightened the effect by painting all the woodwork purple.

Stately Homes

OLD GRANDEUR MEETS NEW IDEAS

These are large houses — the kinds of homes where there are too many rooms to even consider using them all. And the windows are too old not to let in winter drafts, but what does it matter, since fireplaces abound, their flickering light casting deep shadows. In summer, when the hearths are cold, these same windows invite the sun inside to illuminate all the richness and grandeur enjoyed by ages past and generations to come. These handsomely proportioned homes have reassuringly thick walls. Walls that may creak and groan and echo yet always hold fast to their time-worn secrets. The history of a house does not progress at a human pace — it has its own way of changing the people who live within its graceful contours, under generous ceilings. A house with its own illustrious history is a character in its own right. Are we straying from decoration? Not as much as you might think. For decorating a home is perhaps above all an attempt to fathom the secrets of its soul.

AN ANTIQUARIAN'S RICH ABODE

In the Antwerp castle owned by Axel Vervoordt, the famous Belgian antiques dealer, all styles and all periods are welcome, provided that this man of taste has himself chosen the furniture and objects. Each piece is hand-picked and invites reminiscences from every corner of the world. The only criterion is an object's singular aspect, its grace and its rarity. And if the sales he organizes twice a year give him a chance to change decors, his fondness for eclecticism remains unperturbed, whatever is happening around him.

OPPOSITE
The magnificently proportioned swimming pool is fitted with an overflow system that allows the water to drain off at ground level over a wide border of large blue flagstones. The orangery windows were painted in bluish hues, no doubt to compensate for uncertain Belgian skies.

Antwerp, Belgium

OPPOSITE

A beautifully preserved old tile floor and rustic country
furniture adds up to a relaxed look for the guest-house
kitchen, contrasting nicely with the more formal elegance
of the main house. Impromptu family meals and dinners
with close friends are served in this spacious room adjoining
the orangery—much to the delight of all.

OPPOSITE
The far end of the orangery faces one of the estate's
monumental gates while its front windows allow an
unobstructed view of the swimming pool. An old
red brick floor, wicker furniture from southeast
Asia, and a profusion of plants all contribute to
the light yet opulent atmosphere of the place.

ABOVE
Softly lit by the morning light, the small guest room is decorated with a majestic
neoclassical Italian four-poster bed. Perfectly matching the colors of the walls, the Chinese
vase fitted as a lamp sits on a painted Louis XVI console table.

OPPOSITE
From this corner of the orangery one can see the pool and the pool house. Arbors and
trim lawns mark the careful upkeep of the 65-acre grounds.

OPPOSITE
Axel Vervoordt is famous for the variety (and rarity)
of his collections. In this living room, whose
walls were covered in whitewash mixed with iron
oxide, precious ivory objects (Ming dynasty)
decorate the corner of a coffee table made of
bamboo matting (table designed by Axel
Vervoordt). Behind a white-cotton slipcovered
sofa, a collection of Sukhothai pottery.

AN OLD STONE FARM-HOUSE BECOMES A CHEERFUL FAMILY HOME

*Both the main house and the former outbuildings of this
17th-century farm were restored by Yves Taralon to accommodate
family and friends. Today it is a domicile at once open
to all yet still fiercely respectful of its guests' privacy.*

OPPOSITE
Set apart from the main house is a delightful little garden
lodge, in the tradition of the potting shed or summer house.
All around it a small garden designed by Alain Charles
combines exotic grasses, herbs and flowers, mainly in pink.

BELOW
Yves Taralon turned what used to be a large square
farmyard into a topiary garden. To do this the existing
ground had to be carted away and good loam added.
Box hedges and grass were planted to form an old 17th-century
design. All around it, a gravel drive provides access to
all the different buildings now transformed into living quarters.

Touraine, France

ABOVE
This huge yet comfortable living room-cum-library was installed in the attic.
There is no discord between the Louis XVI bed and a modern white-slipcovered sofa. The stairs leading to the
upper level and the wrought-iron railings were made by a craftsman in Angers. Bookshelves of
fir-wood planks dramatically fill the entire wall up to the ceiling.

ABOVE
Upstairs, in a large painted cupboard with recycled wire-mesh doors, a collection
of white earthenware has replaced rare books. The snug intimacy of this room makes it a very pleasant place
for tea, and it is not unusual to find any one of several family members taking
refuge up here to work or daydream.

OPPOSITE
A love of horses is apparent in the entrance hall,
a vast room also used now and then for large
mealtime gatherings. The blond softness of the
formidable beech table by Carlos Scarpa (Forum
Diffusion) is augmented by the Touraine light.
Equestrian prints mounted in modern frames complete
the theme and offset the neutral hues of the walls.

ABOVE
Situated between Toulouse and Carcassonne, the house combines a two-tone color scheme of blue and pink brightens its aspect whatever the season. The 19th-century winter garden invites sunshine all-year round.

OPPOSITE
Palms, clipped honeysuckle (Lonicera nitida) and lavender create an elegant cluster of greenery in front of the glass-paned winter garden.

AN ARTIST'S HOUSE NEAR TOULOUSE

To renovate this castle-sized villa, the painter Fabienne Villacreces gave full vent to her vivid imagination, unhesitatingly working wood, iron and zinc to create a home to match her dreams. The result conveys generosity and inventiveness, attesting to the owner's tremendous creativity and love of life.

FOLLOWING SPREAD
In the veranda, the antique garden furniture seems to have been there forever, between the yellow dazzle of an Abutilon Chinese lantern plant and a bright pink bougainvillea. An 18th-century Korean cupboard is a perfect addition to Géraldine Perrier-Dovon's textiles made specially for Fabienne Villacreces.

ABOVE
Comfort and light are the hallmarks of these two bathrooms. The high-ceilinged
airiness of the upper bathroom contrasts with the artist's garret feel of
the lower one. The modern tub in the smaller bathroom was designed by Philippe
Starck and makes a perfect twosome with the glass cabinet,
once owned by an early 20th-century dentist.

OPPOSITE
Cream walls, an old tiled floor and ultra-classical furnishings for the
dining room. The repatinated draper's cupboard, converted into a buffet, houses its
share of beautiful plates, old glasses and homemade jams. Around the table with
its organdy cloth, a pretty set of 19th-century chairs.

A MAGICAL "PORT OF CALL" IN THE AUBRAC

In this erstwhile hotel set in the very heart of the Auvergne, the designer of the Tartine et Chocolat line of clothes set up a home filled with great ideas and true panache. Her goal? To create a generous and slightly crazy place to entertain in style. A habitat that, like its owner, is singularly difficult to tear yourself away from.

OPPOSITE
In the bathroom of the Crystal Room, twin tubs are set into a pile of volcanic rocks—ideal for two people to have a bath together without getting in each other's way. And the "outdoor" ambiance is sure to refresh.

BELOW
Under the inspired guidance of Catherine Painvin, the Aubrac Annex, a large and somewhat stern-looking house built with volcanic stone, was transformed into a magical hideaway so jaded visitors can leave charmed and renewed.

ABOVE

Nomadic souls are delighted when they come to rest in
the Alexander Room, also known as the Traveler's Room,
a handsome bedroom where one may find old pairs of skis
nuzzling up to photos of elephants and fishing gear.

OPPOSITE

This flawless bedroom seems like the perfect place for falling in
love all over again. White-silk sheets, curtains and a quilted bedspread
(all made in Nepal) make for smooth nights and sunny awakenings.

FOLLOWING SPREAD
Between Auvergne and the Orient, the main living room mixes styles and makes colors come alive.
On the parquet floors Afghan rugs add a vibrant splash of color, flannel-clad cushions
gird low tables, while combination wool-and-cashmere curtains adorn the windows. On the far wall,
shelves were improvised with cinder blocks and old doors.

A FORETASTE
OF ETERNITY

*The Gers is said to be the region of Europe where people
live the longest. When Anne Gayet, a former Parisian
antiques dealer set to work on the remains of a
tumbledown post house left to a century of rack and
ruin, she didn't just import the spirit of Gustavian
style into the bucolic calm of these southerly climes,
she quite simply succeeded in giving eternity a color.*

OPPOSITE
The imposing building stands amid pines,
turned golden in the evening light. Low walls
encircling the house shelter several gardens
planted with palm, olives and roses.

PRECEDING SPREAD, LEFT
In the hall, on beautiful square red tiles, the sideboard was left just as it was. The hefty chestnut staircase is also an original.

PRECEDING SPREAD, RIGHT
The azure-blue softness of the Gustavian style recurs in this large room where a c.1900 pool table takes pride of place. An old pharmacy wall unit serves as bookshelves.

OPPOSITE
Anne Gayet has a taste for beautiful materials and knows better than most how to play with the gentle harmonies of complicated color schemes. In the summer lounge, in front of a Regency fireplace, comfortable sofas (Maison de famille) and a coffee table (Flamant) were designed for convivial moments. In the foreground, a Directoire gaming table and a Louis XV chair.

OPPOSITE
All the floors in the house are outstandingly beautiful. The dining room is designed
in the same tranquil spirit as the rest of the house. Beneath
a late 19th-century bronze-and-crystal chandelier, the dining table is covered
with a quilted cloth (Blanc d'Ivoire).

ABOVE
Looking out onto the swimming pool through elegant French windows, the summer
living room is an ideal spot for savoring a cool moment. The Gustavian table and
bench seat were two great finds in L'Isle-sur-la-Sorgue.

ABOVE
A stunning collection of silver-gilded mirrors brings a touch of opulence to balance the more rustic wood touches. Beneath a 17th-century pier glass, a handsome set of English terra-cotta terrines.

OPPOSITE
In one of the upstairs bedrooms, four late 19th-century chromatographs compare their faded hues. The obelisk doubling as a lamp base comes from L'Isle-sur-la-Sorgue (Quai des Lampes).

A FRENCH-STYLE RETREAT AT NEW YORK CITY'S DOORSTEP

The metamorphosis of these former stables into a small, delightful home reflects the vision of two interior designers who bring very contemporary sensibilities to their design without compromising their natural fondness for French style. All this with a good dose of daring, too.

OPPOSITE
Situated on the edge of a Connecticut forest, this retreat makes a wonderful weekend hideaway for Stephen Sills and his partner James Huniford. At ground level, a large living room and study share virtually the entire floor. Beneath the shingle roof, three bedrooms offer a lovely view over the surrounding trees.

TOP
The unusual gilded four-poster bed, covered in calico with
an 18th-century paisley design becomes an almost sculptural centerpiece and offers
the gilded motif echoed throughout the room.

BELOW
In the vestibule, two starfish mounted in hexagonal frames complement a shell-shaped
ceiling light in white plaster. The naturalist theme extends to the cobbled floor
in the form of three plumes of aloe, made of zinc, "sprouting" beneath the English table,
which displays a Chinese design in the fashion of the early 19th century.

TOP
Shades of gray and white were used in this bedroom to create a
soft and restful atmosphere. In front of the window, a small desk offers a view
into the lush forest just outside.

BELOW
Rough white-marble paving stones cover the floor of the main room which opens
straight onto the grounds through French doors. The decor
here is wonderfully eclectic as illustrated by the Hiquely sculptures set between
two pink-marble columns from Siena, Italy.

Connecticut, U.S.

OPPOSITE

The unusual cobbled main floor is reminiscent of a
winter garden. With an eye to symmetry, a second
bull's-eye window was fitted to the left of the
fireplace, where an 18th-century zinc aloe graces
the mantelpiece. The same white-cotton slipcovers were
used for both the Gustavian chairs and Regency sofas.
The pedestal lamps are by Jean-Michel Frank.

OPPOSITE
The core of the house is formed by a huge
20-foot-high cylinder with large, cambered
glass windows that look out over seven acres
of awe-inspiring grounds. At the back, a small
bridge seems to anchor the ship to shore.

Contemporary Style

LIVING WELL IN THE PRESENT

*People who choose contemporary homes in the country may still harbor a soft spot
for the lean, stark angles of the city, yet no other style brings one closer to nature, with
plenty of windows for pure light, air and open space. If their glass-and-steel
dwellings conjure up cathedrals of futuristic worship more than they do quaint little
cottages, it is quite simply because this transparency, this openness, seems
to them the best way of communing with the natural world that surrounds them.
Following the sun's course across the sky, watching the wind toss the leaves,
or dreaming under a canopy of blue are all pastimes made easy by spare
unencumbered forms. To minimize the boundaries between inside and out and to
bring in maximum light, these rural homeowners not only give shape to their
modern aesthetic but boldly put forth a whole new notion of country living.
When modernity meets the countryside, the result is unforgettable.*

A HOUSE
OF LIGHT

This house, built for a childhood friend by renowned architect Richard Meier,
recalls the prow of a ship gallantly traversing one of the loveliest landscapes New Jersey
has to offer. Designed to bring light to each and every corner, this structure matches
magnificence with grandeur.

OPPOSITE
Austere without being monastic, the simplicity of this immaculate bedroom
adds up to pure elegance. Between a Sam Maloof armchair and a Toshiko Takaezu
sculpture, a single orchid becomes a work of art.

ABOVE
The kitchen is both luminous and functional. Its handsome proportions
make for an even distribution of storage and appliances with room left over for colorful
touches. The slightest ray of sunshine is enough to illumine the large terrace
that functions as an extension of the kitchen.

New Jersey, U.S.

TOP, LEFT
Ceramic pyramid sculptures by William Wyman.

BOTTOM, LEFT
Within this thoroughly transparent construction, careful consideration went into the choice of each ornament. In this house, furniture and objects seem connected by mysterious bonds as powerful as they are invisible. Here, a Hans Wegner valet chair, a Dorothy Gill Barnes basket and a Scott Frances photograph.

TOP, RIGHT
With its cylinders and cubes, the design produced by Richard Meier for these door handles echoes his overall design.

BOTTOM, RIGHT
To reinforce the sense of continuous contact with the surrounding countryside, the architect designed this bathroom to open out onto the woods. The guiding principle of the house is to bring the outside closer for a sense of harmony with the world. The whiteness of the walls and materials, glass and mirrors, emanates the same purity that begins in the bedroom. The collection of pots is by Toshiko Takaezu.

TRANSPARENCY ON A LARGE SCALE

Designed by architect Thomas Phifer, in collaboration with Muriel Brandolini, this impressive "machine for living" is home to a family passionate about the natural world. Located near New York City, in the Hudson River Valley, this glass-and-steel construction offers a 360-degree view over fields of oak and maple forests that blaze with color each fall.

OPPOSITE
Suspended between earth and sky, the house creates a feeling of total symbiosis with the elements. Constantly changing, depending on the time of day and the season, the light here is an architectural component in its own right.

BELOW
The soaring ceilings of the living room are balanced by substantial large-scale furniture. Two sofas covered with Lulu DK's Icon linen and cotton fabric and a Floating Drinks cocktail table designed by Albrizzi succeed brilliantly; the rug is by A.M. Collections.

Upstate New York, U.S.

OPPOSITE

Over a two-year construction period, plans were constantly evolving. What was originally conceived of as a T-shape structure eventually grew into an H. This transformation was crucial for incorporating a screening room, a large office, fitness room and an indoor pool. An outdoor pool, built on the east side of the structure, is encircled by granite paving stones that interact with the lawn to create large geometric patterns. The house retains its human proportions since one cannot see the entire structure from any given angle.

The kitchen features stainless-steel cabinetry; the wood floor and furniture lend
warmth to the space and underscore its connection with the outside.
The Martin Szekely table in birch plywood with attached benches, from Galerie
Kreo, is installed like a sculpture in the breakfast room.

ABOVE
The guest room offers sweeping views of the valley. The carpet, a grid of colored squares, was designed
by Muriel Brandolini and makes the room both welcoming and cheerful.
The Duplex brushed-steel floor lamp and W armchairs are by Andrée Putman for Ecart International.

OPPOSITE
More often than not, Muriel Brandolini works in an intuitive way. Here, she set about bringing the
media room to life by using bright colors and furniture with round, generous shapes. In the screening room,
Lloyd Schwan bookshelves and chaises longues by Pierre Charpin from Galerie Kreo.

AN OLD STONE MILL BECOMES A CATHEDRAL OF GLASS

So as not to betray the spirit of an old mill, which was little more than a ruin, architect Jean-Paul Bonnemaison designed two very different façades. On the village side, stone walls match the church tower, while the other all-glass façade offers unobstructed views of Mont Ventoux and its snow-capped peaks.

OPPOSITE
This house has two distinct parts, one running along a village street and the other, higher side following the contours of the sloping ground. Interspersed with glass-paned walls, natural light pours in through all four living levels throughout the day.

FOLLOWING SPREAD
The interior furnishings were inspired both by Cistercian relics—with nearby Sénanque Abbey providing a magnificent example—and minimalist art. White, a symbol of purity, softens and unifies all the levels. The corner kitchen was installed beneath a wide arch.

Bordeaux, France

AN ORIENTAL OASIS IN BORDEAUX

Two young travelers enthralled with Asia and the lifestyle of the Far East, were keen on reinterpreting an 18th-century Bordeaux mansion by imbuing it with an exotic mystique. The self-taught interior decorator Joanne de Lépinay, crazy about Vietnam and Indonesia, has thoroughly succeeded in meeting her desire for refinement with the flavor of faraway lands.

OPPOSITE
A definite change of scenery in the garden, where the gray cement pool reflects yucca, papyrus and bamboo. The feeling of stability and balance is enhanced by four large ceramic pots (Du Bout du Monde) and the symmetry of the plant beds in front of the stone windbreak.

BELOW
The box bushes atop large zinc pots (Domani) are periodically pruned in rounded contours. On the recliners, fabric from Djakarta.

113

PRECEDING SPREAD, LEFT

In the bedroom, oriental refinement and French elegance co-exist on the best of terms. Behind silk curtains (Jim Thompson), bamboo blinds conjure up Asia. The graceful Fortuny hanging lamps perfectly embody the play between opulent and spare.

PRECEDING SPREAD, RIGHT

In keeping with the house's general theme, the bathroom was rendered in soothing tones. The fittings are in Combrebrune stone from Gironde with a black-granite border.

OPPOSITE

The soft light in the living room is created by translucent blinds over each window, with the added purpose of insulating the room from the street. Most of the objects here have the Far East as their common motif. Framing the fireplace, surmounted by a large wheel on a stand (Asiatides), two elegant Thai urns symbolize perfection.

ON A FRENCH HILLSIDE
LUXURY JAPAN-STYLE

The owner of this enchanting house brings his knowledge of the martial arts and meditation into play with his love of North American wood-frame houses. The two came together in the most congenial manner possible in this stunning yet modest home perched on a quiet, wooded hillside against a backdrop of the peaceful Le Perche region of northwest France.

OPPOSITE
Life is lived here Japanese-style. Meals are served at floor level on a cleverly conceived table with sliding leaves (Galerie Sentou). Parisian architect Sonia Cortese opted for an almost total absence of solid walls between rooms.

ABOVE
The bedroom aspires to achieve a Zen-like attitude. On the floor, rice-straw matting invites bare feet. Ottoman (Forum Diffusion), bamboo and paper lamp (Bô). The damask bedspread is from Caravane.

Le Perche, France

OPPOSITE
From the first designs to the last finishing touches, everything here grew out of the desire to blend with nature. Its beguiling simplicity was attained only with the utmost attention to the smallest of details. In summer, wide eaves protect the house inside from overheating in the ample sunlight.

FOLLOWING SPREAD, LEFT
Wood is the essential element here, its pliant warmth soothes and harmonizes. From the kitchen, a fine view over the Le Perche countryside.

FOLLOWING SPREAD, RIGHT
To heighten the impression of continuity between rooms, the walls never reach full ceiling height and always give way to glass or round apertures.

OPPOSITE

The living room and dining area adjoin the dojo, a small room dedicated to spiritual practices. Radiators are built into the floor and the masonry was designed to store heat during the day and release it at night. In such a minutely conceived structure, one can abandon oneself to the silence stretched out on the raised chaise longue by Christian Ghion (Forum Diffusion).

A RURAL REFUGE FOR TWO DIE-HARD NEW YORKERS

In this distinctly modern house, a museum director and her philosopher husband indulged all of their cherished notions for an ideal second home. The result is a streamlined place diametrically opposed to the let-your-hair down version of the usual country house. Here, the urban look blends seamlessly with the landscape and the functionality associated with city life gives way to an airy and relaxed (and completely elegant) simplicity.

OPPOSITE
The two-bedroom guest house is connected to the main house by a breezeway. A cleverly designed sloping roof dispenses with obtrusive gutters, while allowing rain water to be channeled to a pond at the bottom of the garden.

ABOVE
The ultra-functional master bathroom is floor-to-ceiling white, including flowers and furniture. The floor is paved in glass-mosaic ticle; chrome accents complete the look.

OPPOSITE
When architect Ali C. Hocek embarked on this project, he was well aware that his clients were city people, firmly rooted in a spare urban aesthetic. This greatly influenced his design of the single-level house. A Monica Armani table from Moss on the deck.

FOLLOWING SPREAD
Inside, most of the color comes by way of the artwork, all contemporary, and an integral part of the decor. A painting by Herman Cherry spans the far wall, the painting above the fireplace is by Charles Parness. The living area's sofas and lounge chair are by Poltrona Frau. Saarinen Executive chairs encircle a Mario Bellini table from Cassina.

OPPOSITE
Juan Montoya added a balcony
and terrace to the preexisting sturdy
granite house. As soon as fine
weather arrives, it is here that
Montoya spends his favorite
moments, relaxing and reading
under luxuriant shade trees.

Cabins

MAJESTY AMONG THE TREES

*Cabins are some of the most elemental of structures. In any wooded area
where mature trees are plentiful, homes hewn of wood have existed in some
form throughout recorded history. Perhaps more than any other lodgings, these
country dwellers are marked by their inherent relation to the elements, and
as a result they harmonize to a far greater degree with the landscape from
which they come. Wood, stone, metal and earth all collaborate to form
homes of surprising warmth and stature. No longer simply rustic bumpkins,
these sophisticated cousins to the old-fashioned cabin boast some of the
more innovative techniques of home design, created by people who care
about the quality of (and proximity to) the earth around them.*

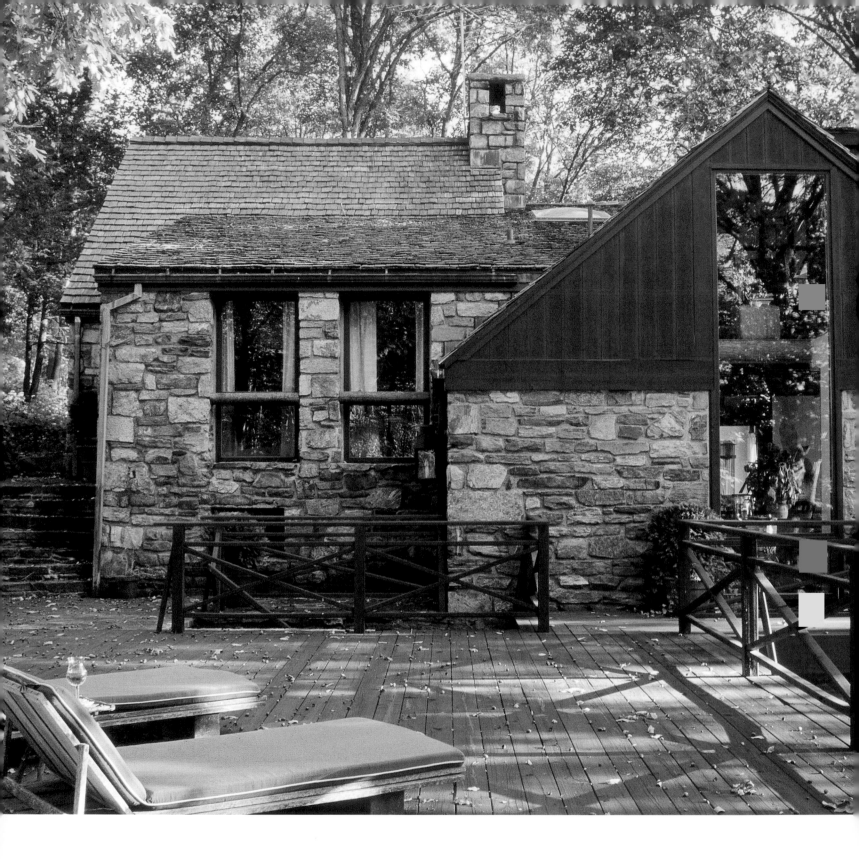

A DREAM HOUSE IN WOOD AND STONE

Decorator Juan Montoya unearthed a forlorn house deep in a forest near the Hudson River, a stone's throw from New York City. From that moment, he knew what he had to do. After major refurbishing work, which gave him a chance to redesign each and every room, the lonely house on the river turned into a wonderful secret retreat, full of books, paintings and antiques — all the trappings of a life well lived.

OPPOSITE AND BELOW

When Montoya discovered this house, it belonged to a hippie community that had constructed its own insular world on the 120-acre grounds. The fittings combine the use of wood, granite and glass, all local materials that help create a total harmony with the forest.

ABOVE

Books are the great passion of the master of this house. The armchairs in front of the
desk designed by Montoya himself are from England and Holland.

An unusual collection of metal and gilded bronze objects go very well with the
old flagstone floor and add a muscular character to the dining room.
But pride of place goes to the lustrous dark-wood table, a country classic whose
simple lines nevertheless impart elegance.

ABOVE

A 19th-century Florentine painting greets visitors in the hall.
Near the sofa, also Italian of the same period, a small mahogany chair from
Ireland holds interesting books.

On the shawl-covered 19th-century table, a miscellany of curious objects have
many different origins. Whether brought back from travels or bought at yard sales,
they create a very cozy atmosphere among books and candles.

FOLLOWING SPREAD

The furniture and lamps in the bedroom were all designed by Juan Montoya.
The bamboo wall coverings bring an Eastern flair. An unusual large model sailboat
evokes all the travels that helped create the wonderful eclecticism that is a
signature of this house.

Upstate New York, U.S.

BELOW
In the well-equipped kitchen, natural materials are given primacy. Slate was used to cover both the floor and the birch-wood work surface. The ceilings of both the dining room and kitchen are made of bamboo.

OPPOSITE
While the black bathroom tiles add a little urban touch, the view over the woods leaves no doubt that you are in the country. A French vase from the 1920s stands out between stainless-steel basins.

BETWEEN LAKE AND FOREST, A PICTURE-PERFECT VIEW

It took no time at all for this matchless view across the wide expanse of Candlewood Lake, in Connecticut, to win over John Frieda, hairdresser to the stars. But the interior of the house wasn't at all to his liking. No matter, interior decorator Sharon Simonaire took things in hand, retaining just the skeleton of the house and, refurbishing all of the rooms.

OPPOSITE
Breakfast, a hallowed moment for city dwellers in the country, is taken on the pier, surveying the majestic sight of trees ablaze with color as Indian summer approaches.

BELOW
The many French windows on the all-wood façade guarantee complete communion with nature.

ABOVE
A loft-style kitchen opens onto the dining room and the living room with a wide walnut buffet that makes a fine
serving area. Generous French windows lend the room a bright and friendly feel.

OPPOSITE
Exposed stonework and varnished wood bring a very cozy atmosphere to the living room, but a splash of
color was needed to warm things up. A footrest covered in blue flannel seemed to fit the bill just right.

FOLLOWING SPREAD
John's bedroom is the largest in the house, and enjoys a
180-degree view of the property. His preference for blond and natural
hues is evident in his choices for furnishings and bedding.
The chest of drawers is flanked by a pair of leather and canvas
bush chairs. At the foot of the bed, an old chest stands
on a wide mat made of sea rushes.

THE LAKE HOUSE

New York publishing executive David Steinberger returned to his childhood summer home when he reclaimed this wood shingle house complete with stunning views over lake and woods. His wife, Dara Caponigro, an editor and designer, tackled the decoration. Her aim: inject the place with a feeling of modernity without trespassing on the cozy spirit dear to David's heart.

OPPOSITE
In warm, fine weather, much time is wiled away on the porch, where a view over the lake provides a refreshing change of scenery. The table and chairs are vintage Richard Schultz designs for Knoll. Dara Caponigro gave a place of honor to a 1960s molded-plastic armchair that came from her childhood home.

BELOW

With her preference for muted colors, Caponigro chose whites, grays and beiges for the indoor decoration. In the dining area, the Alzaia light is by Fontana Arte.

OPPOSITE

The floor and ceiling of the sunsplashed master bedroom are painted white. With a nod to the surrounding woodland, the ottomans are covered in a delicate fern-motif fabric by Old World Weavers.

FOLLOWING SPREAD

The large fireplace lets the family make the most of its lovely "cabin," summer and winter alike. Each season provides plenty of branches and flowers to complement the natural tones of the decor. The living room features a Cannes sofa by Crate & Barrel and a wicker ottoman by Bielecky Bros.

MODERN VARIATIONS IN NORMANDY

It began with the purchase of a typical Normandy cottage in the heart of the Auge region. But as the family grew, attempts to fit into the little house were in vain. Finally everyone agreed to build a modern all-wood dwelling in the style of Canadian far north. The cows still haven't got over it...

OPPOSITE
The earth tones of the kitchen-dining room, painted in shades of sienna and red ocher, lend it year-round warmth. The fireplace has been raised so the flames can be seen (and felt) at mealtimes.

BELOW
The wooden shutters open to give the guest bathroom a view to the front yard. Unique inside shutters can be closed for privacy.

ABOVE AND OPPOSITE
The house was designed by architect Gérard Colard and built
in six months by local craftsmen. It resembles a self-contained hamlet
made up of interlocking cells. To the north, the shingle roof extends
very low toward the ground, keeping the house snug and warm in
cold weather. Depending on its exposure, red cedar will fade
gracefully as it ages, in shades varying from pale russet to dark gray.

FOLLOWING SPREAD
Originally built to minimize trips to the seaside, the pool
is just about everyone's favorite room. Interior designer Martine
Dufour had the bright idea of covering it with an industrial
greenhouse to keep it light and airy while protecting it from
the elements. The indoor temperature is adjusted automatically
according to the outdoor conditions.

RE-CREATING NEW ENGLAND IN THE OLD WORLD

Faithful to the austere and symmetrical architectural spirit so prevalent on the East Coast of the United States, this ultra-functional house in the Brabant-Walloon region of Belgium was built in record time. Perfectly balanced forms and an abundance of indoor light are the main features of this structure with its combination of pine, cedar and oak.

OPPOSITE
Architects Pierre Hoet and Jean Massa make no secret of their admiration for New England homes. With a 65-foot-long veranda running the length of the façade, you would hardly think you were in the Belgian countryside. The roof of flat slate tiles look amazingly like shingles, a favorite roofing material on the other side of the Atlantic.

Brabant-Walloon, Belgium

BELOW
The wondrously bright dining room makes no excuses when it comes to whiteness. The Pausa seats (Flexform) and the glass-fronted Piroscafo cupboard (Molteni) stand on a bleached oak-parquet floor.

The same simplicity extends to the bedroom. Between the wall lights (Manufactor), a row of family photos. All the windows in the house are sash windows, New England-style.

OPPOSITE
Architect Pierre Hoet made the fireplace and coffee table himself, around which simple sofas (Padova) create a convivial atmosphere. The beautiful windows allow the natural surroundings to become an integral part of the decor.

FOLLOWING SPREAD
The huge kitchen is every bit a match for those spacious American kitchens. Planned for informal meals, it has all the functional features which make you want to roll up your sleeves and start cooking. Around the table lit by a Naviglio ceiling light, the upholstered Mixer seats (Flexform) are the only splash of color in the room.

OPPOSITE
Set in the midst of vineyards, Agnès Comar's
house comes into view at the end of a drive lined
by impressive plane trees. Depending on the
time of day, the whitewashed walls reveal
contrasting hues with ocher predominating.

Mediterranean Style

DECORATION WITH SOUTHERN ACCENTS

*To escape the unrelenting gray of northern Europe, some people have opted for the
south and its warm, sunny mornings. Living outdoors, forgetting all about rain,
daydreaming by a pool amid lavender and rosemary, dining with friends
beneath the arbor: who can resist the lure of these images of endless vacations?
Leaving Normandy and Brittany to people who like changing skies, those whose
eyes only truly come alive when they get south of the Loire don't do things by
halves when it comes to creating their fantasy home in settings just this side of
paradise. So many brightly colored regions in southern France full of homes
with an infinite variety of styles — from farmhouses nestling beneath cypress trees
or lost amid vines and olive boughs, to majestic villas exuding patrician
exclusivity — each home celebrates a dolce vita with the sun as its witness.*

AT HOME WITH FASHION DESIGNER AGNĒS COMAR

Agnès Comar has set up home in the Lubéron region of France in an old "tawery," a place where tallow for candles was once whitened. Dating from the 18th century, this noble dwelling favors light atmospheres for all its rooms, which are at once both simple and sophisticated.

OPPOSITE
Virginia creeper spreads over an arbor creating a sun-dappled shade, even at high noon. The setting is particularly pleasant and everyone enjoys this cool nook, be it over lunch or as the perfect spot to indulge in a long, quiet siesta.

ABOVE
In the middle of the kitchen-dining room, with its pale yellow walls, the centerpiece
is a beautiful Bordeaux table (designed by Anne-Cécile Comar) surrounded by chairs
that were stripped and repainted in country white.

The bathroom sinks and the surfaces surrounding the bathtub were created with "shrimp-pink" cement,
a color that goes well with the fennel-green walls. The curtains are in light
cotton terry. The kindly gaze of the caryatid, designed by Michel Biehn, surveys these rooms
all dedicated to its inhabitants' well-being.

OPPOSITE
The bedroom is a celebration of white: a white four-poster bed, designed by Agnès Comar in
painted beech wood; white bed linens, white bedspread trimmed with fennel-colored braid and
white curtains in organdy. All add up to a sophisticated and peaceful refuge.

COLOR FIRST AND FOREMOST...

Throughout their professional lives — one devoted to fashion, the other to film — Irène and Giorgio Silvagni have had a thousand and one opportunities to express their artistic temperaments and creative fantasies. A Bohemian spirit fills their Provençal farmhouse, a "ruin for sale" that had not been lived in for a hundred years, but which captured their hearts the moment they saw it.

OPPOSITE
A keen admirer of the Villa Medici, Giorgio painted the interiors himself, mixing pigments as the spirit moved him, or as the room's exposure dictated. The dark-hued wood of the Thonet chairs at the foot of the homemade bed bring an elegant contrast to the Matisse-blue walls.

Provence, France

OPPOSITE

It is hard to believe this garden was abandoned for so long. Olives, palms and various fruit trees have been planted around the pool nicknamed "The Unkind Pond" (La Désobligeante) because of its narrowness, best suited for solitary swims. In the height of summer, all this foliage guarantees a welcome coolness.

BELOW

Set amid prolific greenery, the farm partakes in a kind of hide-and-seek game of light and shade. The shutters were painted blue, a tribute to the blue of sea and sky.

FOLLOWING SPREAD
The antique curtains in the dining room beautifully
complement the Roussillon ocher of the walls, while
a quilted Provençal cloth brightens the table.
On winter evenings, the candles in the candelabra
and the lamps bring a romantic touch to dinner.

PIERRE BERGĒ'S PARADISE FOUND

Pierre Bergé discovered the village house of his dreams in Saint-Rémy-de-Provence where the inhabitants have remained true to their roots. Out of this 18th-century country home, with the talent for which he is well known, Bergé created a quiet refuge where he can surround himself with friends. Well removed from the hubbub of Paris, he comes here as often as possible to find new inspiration.

OPPOSITE
All around the ocher-stained pool house, large jardinières with olive trees cast their silvery reflection on the surface of the water. On either side of the pool, lined with lavender and cypress, recliners and parasols (Le Cèdre Rouge) beckon guests for an afternoon of pure relaxation. Instant magic.

Provence, France

OPPOSITE

Forming a double hedge along the walk linking the garden to the pool, hibiscus plants in terra-cotta pots provide a stunning display of flowers all summer long. For the patio, old flagstones and fine gravel.

BELOW

Even if Pierre Bergé had a pretty clear idea of what he wanted, he could not have done without the valuable help of landscape gardener Michel Semini and architect Hugues Bosc. Apart from the Chinese mulberry tree (on the right), that was there from the start, all the trees were planted as adult specimens to create the impression of an old garden.

Provence, France

OPPOSITE
The bedroom floor tiles (Didier Gruel) were cleverly laid
to resemble a carpet. A painted metal bed (Estelle
Garcin) and old wicker armchair (Xavier Nicod,
L'Isle-sur-la-Sorgue) are in the same muted pastel tones.
In the corridor, the star-shaped ceiling light made of
painted paper was designed by Tom Dixon.

A DREAM HOUSE
ON THE RIVER'S EDGE

*A house as only children draw them: square, thoroughly symmetrical, with a door
in the center, windows in neat lines, and a steep sloping roof. The day painter Bernard Dufour and
his wife, interior designer Martine Dufour, glimpsed this house's silhouette
in the midst of its luxuriant trees and gardens, they were both head over heels. Like a dream long
nurtured, theirs finally came true on the banks of the Lot.*

ABOVE
Siestas are oh so sweet in this "Miss Eliett" 19th-century beach chair made of Rubelli fabric
and the imagination flows freely. A perfect spot for an artist nurturing new ideas.

OPPOSITE
The house, with its splendid roof of scaled slate tiles typical of the region comes into
view at the end of a double raw of pruned box hedges. Thick stone walls keep the rooms
delightfully cool, even on the hottest summer days.

ABOVE
This quintessential early 19th-century home has kept
its authentic feel—one could almost be transported
back in time. A large walnut table, opposite the huge
dining room fireplace was designed by Bernard.

OPPOSITE
The owners of this house spent plenty of time choosing
colors; all the rooms were whitewashed using local pigments.
The billiard room features a Charles X billiard table with lion's
heads and a painting by Bernard above the mantelpiece.

FOLLOWING SPREAD
Built in 1814, the old cowshed is so roomy that it can
be used to store firewood and some of the painter's
supplies. The old chesterfield may seem worn out,
but it still surveys the canvases with a critical eye.

BETWEEN WARM STONE AND LAVENDER

Nestled at the foot of the Lubéron range in outstanding natural surroundings, this old farmhouse has found ways, down through the centuries, of turning its weekend guests into full-time residents. It's easy to see how this magnificent setting casts a spell on all who see it.

OPPOSITE
From one year to the next outbuildings were added to the original house to create its unique stepped contours. Amid ilex, pine, cypress, bay laurel, rosemary and olive, the house is now firmly anchored in the landscape.

BELOW
Landscape gardener Michel Semini had the bold idea of setting the swimming pool among 2,000 lavender bushes inventively pruned to form globes. The garden is deliberately devoid of flowers, instead paying tribute to the dryer more durable plants that surround it.

FOLLOWING SPREAD
Painted in straw tones, the bedroom is an impressive size—a huge loft, it comfortably serves as office and TV room as well. Large terra-cotta tiles were chosen for the floor accented with rattan matting.

ABOVE, LEFT AND RIGHT
The winter living room was designed by Michèle Belaiche, mistress of the house,
who was keen to live all year round surrounded by pine trees. On the mantelpiece, Timorese
drums. On either side of the fireplace, a pair of lovely old Provençal
armchairs. To hide the radiator, Michèle designed the fanned oak screen herself.
Large windows offer outstanding views over the trees.

PROVENCE, ENGLISH-STYLE

Reflecting the tastes of its British owners and the talents of a trio of architects, this country home built in the 1960s has matured beautifully in tune with the seasons. A stone's throw from St. Paul-de-Vence, this country hideout offers its inhabitants an incomparable lifestyle in the midst of nature.

OPPOSITE
Like all the houses in this area, this single-level country home was built entirely of stone. The garden was created by landscape designer Jean Mus in perfect harmony with the surrounding landscape.

ABOVE, LEFT AND RIGHT
More an outdoor living room than a terrace, this peaceful terrace acts as a link
between house and pool. Furnished with white canvas cushions,
the stone benches are deep enough to sit back in voluptuous repose. In summer,
its shade delights readers or those seeking a cool place for drinks,
and when evenings turn cooler, the fireplace makes autumn a welcome time. The
lamps are Indian urns with iron shades made by a local craftsman.

ABOVE
The children's room is decorated to resemble a boat's cabin
or fisherman's hut. Covered with wood-plank paneling painted
in sky blue, the walls give the room a warm and welcoming
feeling. The bunk beds are in hazel wood.

OPPOSITE
Done up with simple good taste, the bathtub allows a clear view
to the forest (and a sun-drenched bath). Clean, symmetrical
forms and a palette of mostly white help maximize the space.
All add up to ultimate comfort in a small space.

TIME RECOVERED
BENEATH PLANE TREES

*Near St. Rémy-de-Provence, a family of stone enthusiasts
turned this forgotten farmhouse into a garden of Eden
skillfully divided between mineral and vegetable. While father
and son plunged into impressive restoration projects,
landscape gardener Dominique Lafourcade created
a garden in tune with the surrounding landscape.*

OPPOSITE
In the shade of two venerable plane trees, this impressive 18th-century
bastide farmhouse left its heyday behind when all its shutters were
closed and it sank into oblivion. Nowadays, family and friends come in
droves to make new memories behind its welcoming threshold.

BELOW
In front of the fountain in the herb garden, a bed hemmed by pruned box
contains basil, chives, parsley and tarragon. The garden's central theme
is its many shades of silvery green As for flowers, climbing roses, wisteria
and oleander, are all seen to their best advantage in this setting.

ABOVE
Painted a dove gray that is as understated as it is elegant, the kitchen is both
convivial and functional. Unearthed in local bric-a-brac shops, old pottery and bottles
add to its earthy charm. The table is 19th-century oak, the chairs rattan.

OPPOSITE
Auction rooms and antique shops in Avignon, Arles and Nîmes are gold mines
for bargain hunters. In this well-lit bedroom, an English brass bed and prints of the Greek
philosophers create a classic atmosphere that is just right.

FOLLOWING SPREAD
The eclecticism that prevails in the living room decoration
shows a confident eye and a mastery of harmonies.
A tabletop was made-to-measure to bring new life to a
pair of old joiner's trestles. Two olive pots were ingeniously
transformed into lamps. On the left, a chest from an
old sacristy, once used for storing cassocks.

THE EMBROIDERER'S ENCHANTED CASTLE

Edith Mézard lives and works in the Château de l'Ange — Castle of the Angel — in the small village of Lumières, on the edge of the Lubéron. Behind the fine pink-ocher façade, the famous embroiderer dedicates this bewitching place to the hues and textures of Italy. Dolce vita guaranteed....

ABOVE
Contrasting shades of red give the thick walls nobility and character. The cat, doubling as sentinel, assumes its duties with light-footed grace.

OPPOSITE
A path lined with cypress trees emphasizes the architecture of the façade and lends the air of a Tuscan villa. Climbing roses frame the front door on the garden side and suffuse the rooms with an irresistible aroma.

Lubéron, France

OPPOSITE
The summer dining room leads straight out into the garden. Around the large farmhouse table are old wood-slat garden chairs, their backs and seats covered with linen cushions for all-around comfort.

ABOVE
Hues of white and beige for the small library and sitting room. A coffee table by Jacqueline Morabito, lamp by Andrée Putman, and sofa by Yves Halard covered with a striped cotton ticking.

The kitchen, where family meals are served, is one of the house's central rooms. Designed by Michel Biehn, the storage units consist of built-in wicker drawers that match the dining chairs. Pots of aromatic plants ensure a constant supply of herbs.

FOLLOWING SPREAD
In the large living room with its classical elegance, a gilded wooden arrow, a decorative feature in the room, was unearthed in Michel Biehn's shop in L'Isle-sur-la-Sorgue. His shop also provided the little 19th-century Italian chair in gilded wood pictured in the foreground. The raw linen curtains are by Robert le Héros.

ACKNOWLEDGMENTS

The homeowners, designers and architects who welcomed ELLE DECOR
for the stories seen on these pages:

Michèle Belaiche, Pierre Bergé, Jean-Paul Bonnemaison, Muriel Brandolini, Pierre Brinon,
Dara Caponigro, Anthony Collett, Agnès Comar, Sonia Cortesse, Bernard Dufour, John Frieda, Anne Gayet,
Brian Godbold, Sandy and Lou Grotta, Ali C. Hocek, Pierre Hoet, James Huniford, Marin Karmitz,
Alexandre, Bruno and Dominique Lafourcade, Edmund Leites, Joanne de Lépinay,
Jean Massa, Mr. and Mrs. Mayer, Richard Meier, Edith Mézard,
Mi Casa, Juan Montoya, Catherine Painvin, Thomas Phifer, Julie Prisca, Stephen Sills, Irène
and Giorgio Silvagni, Rochelle Slovin, John Stefanidis, Yves Taralon, Axel Vervoordt,
Fabienne Villacreces, Andrew Zarzycki.

And all those who wish to remain anonymous.

CREDITS

PHOTOGRAPHS BY
Fernando Bengoechea: pp. 126–131.
Gilles de Chabaneix: pp. 184–189. **Vera Cruz**: pp. 190–195. **Jérôme Darblay**: pp. 70–75.
Jacques Dirand: pp. 154–159, 208–213. **Scott Frances**: pp. 100, 102–103. **Patrice de Grandry**: back cover, bottom right; pp. 118–125.
Marianne Haas: back cover, top right; pp. 28–37, 64–69, 132–141, 142–147, 166–171, 172–177,
178–183, 202–207. **Jean-Luc Laloux**: back cover, bottom left; pp. 160–165. **Guillaume de Laubier**: cover; back cover, top left, center left;
pp. 4, 8–13, 14–21, 22–27, 38–43, 44–55, 56–63, 86–91, 92–99, 112–117, 196–201.
Nicolas Mathéus: pp. 108–111. **Laura Resen**: pp. 148–153. **Gilles Trillard**: pp. 75–85.
William Waldron: pp. 101, 104–107.

STORIES PRODUCED BY
François Baudot: back cover, top right; pp. 28–37, 86–91. **Marie-Claire Blanckaert**: cover; back cover, bottom right, center left;
pp. 8–13, 14–21, 22–27, 44–55, 56–63, 70–75, 76–85, 92–99, 132–141, 142–147,
166–171, 172–177, 178–183, 190–195, 196–201, 202–207. **Michael Boodro**: pp. 100–107. **Franck Descombes**:
back cover, bottom left; pp. 160–165. **Geneviève Dortignac**: pp. 112–117. **Laurence Dougier**: pp. 108–111. **Marie-Claude Dumoulin**:
pp. 184–189. **Armel Ferroudj-Bégou**: pp. 118–125. **Alice Hanson**: pp. 4, 38–43. **Marie Kalt**: pp. 208–213.
Jesse Kornbluth: pp. 126–131. **Françoise Labro**: pp. 154–159.
Mitchell Owens: pp. 148–153. **Laure Verchère**: pp. 64–69.

ELLE DECOR (U.S.) and ELLE DECORATION (France) are both imprints of the Hachette Filipacchi Media group.
The content of this book was taken from ELLE DECOR and ELLE DECORATION.